Who Will You Be When You Grow Up?

MOLLY POTTER

ILLUSTRATED BY
SARAH JENNINGS

BLOOMSBURY EDUCATION

LONDON   OXFORD   NEW YORK   NEW DELHI   SYDNEY

This book is dedicated to my extraordinary and brilliant friend Hazel Marsh who worked out what she wanted to do when she grew up: save the world, make cakes out of weird ingredients and play second fiddle :)

BLOOMSBURY EDUCATION
Bloomsbury Publishing Plc
50 Bedford Square, London, WC1B 3DP, UK
Bloomsbury Publishing Ireland Limited
29 Earlsfort Terrace, Dublin 2, D02 AY28, Ireland
BLOOMSBURY, BLOOMSBURY EDUCATION and the Diana logo are trademarks of Bloomsbury Publishing Plc
First published in Great Britain, 2026 by Bloomsbury Publishing Plc
Text copyright © Molly Potter, 2026
Illustrations copyright © Sarah Jennings, 2026

A catalogue record for this book is available from the British Library

ISBN: HB: 978-1-8019-9349-4; ePub: 978-1-8019-9347-0

2 4 6 8 10 9 7 5 3 1

Printed and bound in China by Leo Paper Products, Heshan, Guangdong

To find out more about our authors and books visit www.bloomsbury.com and sign up for our newsletters
For product safety related questions contact productsafety@bloomsbury.com

Who Will You Be When You Grow Up?

Have you ever thought about the future and what your life will look like when you're an adult? There are so many different possibilities, it's fun to imagine.

This book asks lots of questions to get you thinking about what you want to be like when you're older. It will ask you about...

- activities you would like to try

- places you might like to visit

- choices you could make.

After exploring this book, the next time a grown up asks about your dreams for the future, you'll have loads of ideas!

When I grow up, I want to be kind, have three large pet dogs, live in the countryside and ride a camel!

Contents

What will you be like?

What will you enjoy doing?

What will you do to stay healthy?

What will your friends be like?

Where will you live?

What unusual things might you try?

What might you be really good at?

Turn to page 18.

What adventures might you have?

Turn to page 20.

What might people say about you?

Turn to page 22.

What kind of job will you have?

Turn to page 24.

What life experiences will you have?

Turn to page 26.

What will make you happy?

Turn to page 28.

What will you be like?

The person you become will depend on lots of different things, such as what you believe is important, what the adults in your life are like, the chances you get and the choices you make.
Will you...

Be tidy or messy?

Be serious or silly?

Talk a lot or prefer to listen?

Be adventurous or enjoy staying at home?

Follow the rules or make up your own rules?

Prefer to make plans or be happy to just see what happens?

Dress smartly or not worry too much about what you wear?

Just think about yourself or enjoy helping others?

Which of these are you most certain about?

7

What will you enjoy doing?

When you grow up you might enjoy doing hobbies in your free time. Hobbies are activities we love to do again and again. Do you think you will like any of these?

Playing sport?

Cooking?

Playing board games?

Painting pictures?

Going to the cinema?

Collecting things?

Knitting?

Singing in a choir?

Taking photos?

Fishing?

Gardening?

Looking after animals?

Doing puzzles?

Can you think of other hobbies you might like?

What will you do to stay healthy?

There are lots of things you can do that will help you stay fit, healthy and feeling great! Which seem like the most fun or the easiest to keep doing as you grow up?

Playing sport?

Eating lots of vegetables?

Going for long walks?

Drinking plenty of water?

Getting outdoors every day?

Eating plenty of fruit?

Laughing a lot?
(it's good for you!)

Ha, ha! Hee, hee!

Getting enough sleep?

Going for a run?

Taking time to relax?

Going to the dentist to keep your teeth healthy?

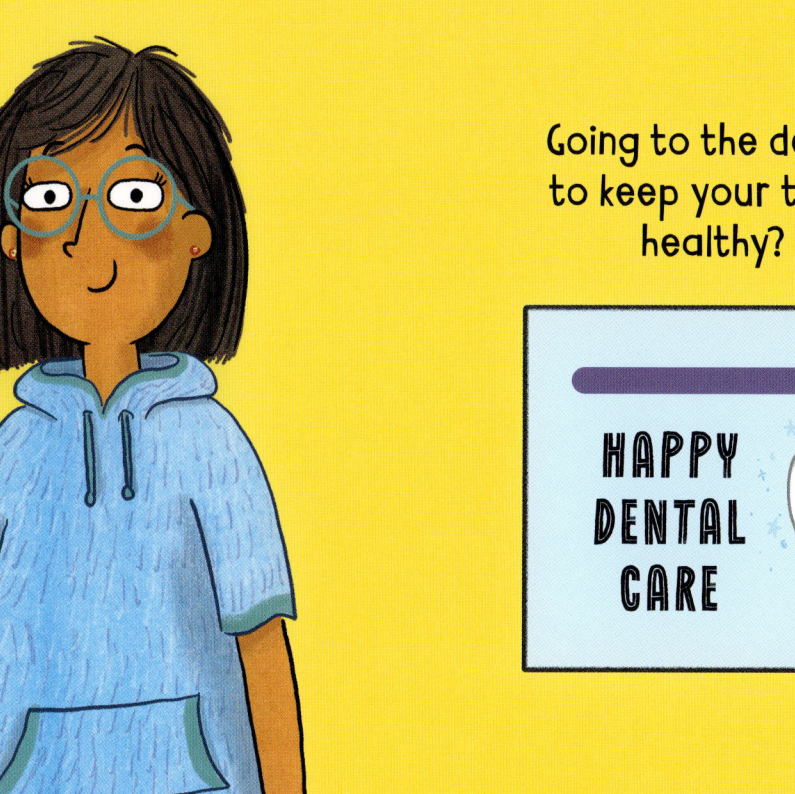

HAPPY DENTAL CARE

Going swimming regularly?

Looking after our bodies can help us to feel livelier and happier.

11

What will your friends be like?

Friends are great to have. They can help us, teach us, make us feel good about ourselves and be fun to spend time with. When you grow up, do you hope to have friends who...

Make you laugh?

Don't always agree with you?

Forgive you when you make a mistake?

Listen to you?

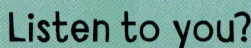

Make you feel like they really care about you?

Want to spend a lot of time with you?

Same time tomorrow?

I made this card to cheer you up.

YOU STAR!

Make time to help you when you're struggling?

Will you have...
- friends of different ages?

- friends who like doing the same things as you?

- lots of friends or a just a few really close ones?

When you grow up, what do you think will make YOU a good friend?

13

Where will you 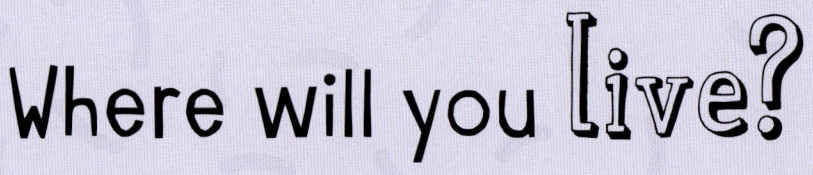?

Some people live in the same place for their whole lives, while others live in many different homes. Where do you think you'll end up living?

In a small house near the sea?

Not in a house, but in a caravan or on a boat?

In an old house in the countryside, with no neighbours?

14

In a big house in a town?

In an apartment in the city, surrounded by lots of neighbours?

In an unusual looking house with lots of floors?

In a house that you designed and built yourself?

Every home is different. Some people choose to live with friends, some with their family and some people live on their own.

15

What unusual things might you try?

Sometimes, we get a chance to do something unusual that not everyone gets to do. This can be really exciting and make great memories. Do you think you will try any of these?

A parachute jump?

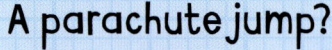

Performing on stage?

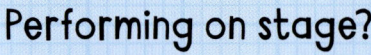

Living in another country for a while?

Running a marathon?

Writing a book?

Taking a trip in a hot air balloon?

Learning to juggle
or walk a tightrope?

Seeing the northern lights?

WOW!

Riding a camel?

Going scuba diving?

Can you think of any more
unusual things you might
like to try?

What might you be really good at?

Most people are good at some things and not so good at others. We usually enjoy doing things that we find easy but it can be fun to challenge ourselves to get better at things we find difficult. Which of these things are you already good at and which would you like to get better at, as you grow up?

Dancing?

Fixing things?

Having lots of ideas?

Making people laugh?

Adding up numbers quickly?

$$4 + 5 + 16 + 24 + 8 + 45 + 10 + 2 =$$

18

19

What adventures might you have?

Adventures are unusual and exciting journeys. Adventures can be challenging – in a good way! Would you like to go on any of these adventures?

A really long walk
that lasts several days?

Climb a mountain?

Canoe down a river?

Go on a long horse ride?

See big animals in the wild?

Visit somewhere few people go to, like the north or south pole, a desert, the middle of an ocean or a rainforest?

Travel around the world?

Some people search for adventure more than others. If you're someone who prefers to stay closer to home – that's totally fine too.

What might people **say** about **you?**

Which of these compliments do you think you'd most like to hear from people when you're a grown up?

23

What kind of job will you have?

Most grown-ups have a job that helps them pay for everything they need. It's great if the job you have includes things you enjoy. Would you like...

To work indoors or outdoors?

To work alone or with other people?

A job that helps other people?

A job fixing things?

A job making things?

A job at the same place each day, or one that takes you to different places?

I work in the same room every day, but every day feels different.

A job where you use your brain and investigate?

To be the boss or be told what to do?

Can you put these boxes in the store room please.

Many people have lots of different jobs in their lifetime, while some people do the same job all their lives.

What life experiences will you have?

There are some experiences in life that many people have, but not everyone will experience them all. Which of the following do you think you will probably do?

Learn to drive?

Learn to cook?

Go to college or university?

I'm off to learn even more.

Live in the place where you grew up or try somewhere new?

Fall in love?

Own a pet?

Fetch!

Buy a house?

Have children?

We can never know exactly how our lives will turn out. What we hope for as a child might change as we grow up.

27

What will make you happy?

The things that make us happy can change as we get older. Which of the following do you think will be the most important for a happy life as a grown-up?

Good friends

Finding things you love to do

Being kind to other people

What do I think will make me happy?

People who really love you

Feeling useful

Exciting holidays

A job you really enjoy

Becoming an expert in something

Learning how to enjoy each moment

Earning lots of money

Finding fun in new challenges

Being thankful for everything you have

Once you've decided what makes you happy, ask your friends and family what makes them happy. You'll probably get lots of different answers!

Notes for PARENTS, CARERS and TEACHERS

Growing up

As children grow up, their increasing self-reliance means that adults need to adapt how they support them: moving from a baby who needs all their needs met, to a young adult that eventually leaves home equipped to face the world.

Discussing a child's possible future can be part of this 'equipping'. Exploring ideas about the future with a child can plant seeds and help them to realise that you are interested in their future, which can be validating and reassuring, and raise their aspirations.

You could discuss:

- What activities and games you enjoyed as a child and then how this changed as you grew up

- What you were like as a child and which childhood traits you still have

- What you wanted to be when you grew up – if you knew

- How becoming a teenager might have changed your relationships with your parents or carers

- What you found difficult about growing up and what you liked about it.

Discussing growing up

Children often want to be more grown-up than they currently are. However, at the same time, the changes that happen as you get older such as being more responsible, making bigger decisions and becoming more independent, can seem daunting and lead to feelings of anxiety for some children.

For this reason, it's really helpful when adults can honestly share their own experiences of being a young child and growing up.

Considering children's futures

You can help children feel excited about exploring new opportunities, trying new things and discovering their passions by showing a keen interest. Encourage short-lived interests and long-term pursuits equally, as they all contribute to self-awareness and confidence.

When talking about the future, it's important to help children understand that change is inevitable and it's normal to find life challenging at times. These challenges give children the opportunity to show themselves what they are capable of, that they can adapt and cope, which increases their resilience and helps them grow.

Worry and anxiety about change

Anticipating the changes of growing up might cause us to worry and feel anxious. Here are some important things to remember about anxiety:

- It's normal to worry when facing the uncertainty created by life's many changes.

- Finding out more information about something that's triggering anxiety can help us to feel better.

- We feel anxious when we believe we won't cope with a new task or upcoming change. However, we nearly always do cope even when things don't go to plan! It can help to try and remember times that we have overcome a daunting task, to prove to ourselves that we can cope.

- Less helpful aspects of anxiety include ruminating (thinking the same unhelpful worry over and over again) and catastrophising (believing that everything that could go wrong, will go wrong). Helping children to become aware of these tendencies and finding ways that they can challenge these thoughts can help reduce their anxiety.

- It's unwise to avoid everything that triggers anxiety as it reinforces the idea that something is scary and so we will continue trying to avoid it. When we face things that make us anxious, we prove to ourselves that we can cope. Many things that cause us to feel anxious are worth doing in the long run, for example learning to swim or trying something for the first time.

- Our modern lives are filled with so many readily available rewards such as sugary treats and screen time, which, when consumed too regularly, can lead to overstimulation, increased anxiety and low mood. Encourage your child to explore other healthier ways of managing uncomfortable emotions (like boredom). Find activities that help them relax without relying so often on immediate rewards. This helps with positive mental health.

- When children are worrying, resist jumping in with solutions. Listen attentively and validate their feelings. Speculating gently about what they're feeling can open up dialogue that helps them process and solve their own problems. Every time they solve their own problems, their anxiety is reduced as they prove to themselves that they can cope.

Let's imagine the future...

Here are some questions for you to answer now. Why not check back in six months, a year, five, or even ten years' time to see if you have changed your mind!

1 What words do you hope people will use to describe you?

5 What do you think will make you most happy?

2 What kind of job would you like?

6 Can you name a place you would love to visit or a journey you think you will take?

3 What hobbies would you like to have?

7 What do you think you'll be good at?

4 What unusual thing or adventure would you love to try?

8 Do you think you'll find it easy to stay fit and eat healthily?

When someone next asks you who you want to be when you grow up, you'll have lots to tell them!